W9-CYE-662

WHAT ARE WEATHER INSTRUMENTS?

JOSEPH KAMPFF

Britannica®
Educational Publishing

IN ASSOCIATION WITH

ROSEN
EDUCATIONAL SERVICES

Published in 2015 by Britannica Educational Publishing (a trademark of Encyclopædia Britannica, Inc.) in association with The Rosen Publishing Group, Inc.
29 East 21st Street, New York, NY 10010

Copyright © 2015 The Rosen Publishing Group, Inc., and Encyclopædia Britannica, Inc. Encyclopædia Britannica, Britannica, and the Thistle logo are registered trademarks of Encyclopædia Britannica, Inc. All rights reserved.
Distributed exclusively by Rosen Publishing.
To see additional Britannica Educational Publishing titles, go to rosenpublishing.com.

First Edition

Britannica Educational Publishing
J. E. Luebering: Director, Core Reference Group
Mary Rose McCudden: Editor, Britannica Student Encyclopedia

Rosen Publishing
Hope Lourie Killcoyne: Executive Editor
Nelson Sá: Art Director
Michael Moy: Designer
Cindy Reiman: Photography Manager

Library of Congress Cataloging-in-Publication Data

Kampff, Joseph.
What are weather instruments?/Joseph Kampff. —First edition.
    pages cm—(Let's find out! Weather)
Includes bibliographical references and index.
ISBN 978-1-62275-791-6 (library bound) — ISBN 978-1-62275-792-3 (pbk.) —
ISBN 978-1-62275-793-0 (6-pack)
1. Meteorological instruments—Juvenile literature. 2. Weather—Juvenile literature. I. Title.
QC876.K34 2015
551.5028'4—dc23

Manufactured in the United States of America

Cover, p. 1 OlegDoroshin/Shutterstock.com (hand with thermometer), Zorandim/Shutterstock.com (wind meter);
p. 4 Ciaran Griffin/Stockbyte/Thinkstock; p. 5 Jim Reed/Photo Researchers/Getty Images; p. 6 Science Source/
Photo Researchers/Getty Images; p. 7 Myotis/Shutterstock.com; pp. 8-9 Svend77/Shutterstock.com; p. 9 Science &
Society Picture Library/Getty Images; p. 10 grafvision/iStock/Thinkstock; p. 11 Frances M. Roberts/Newscom; p. 12
BMJ/Shutterstock.com; pp. 13, 15 Fuse/Thinkstock; p. 14 Julius Kiesekamp/iStock/Thinkstock; p. 16 Encyclopædia
Britannica, Inc.; p. 17 Minerva Studio/iStock/Thinkstock; p. 18 DVIDS/Navy Media Content Services; p. 19 David R.
Frazier/DanitaDelimont.com/Danita Delimont Photography/Newscom; p. 20 chatchaisurakram/iStock/Thinkstock;
p. 21 NOAA/Forrest M. Mims III; p. 22 Print Collector/Hulton Archive/Getty Images; p. 23 DVIDS/NASA/Paul E. Alers;
pp. 24, 25 NASA; p. 26 U.S. Air Force photo by A1C Jaeda Waffer/DVIDS; pp. 26-27 jerbarber/iStock/Thinkstock;
pp. 28, 29 © David Young-Wolff/PhotoEdit; interior pages background image solarseven/Shutterstock.com.

CONTENTS

TALKING ABOUT THE WEATHER

The weather is one of the most common topics of conversation. Most people make casual remarks about the weather, and that is enough for most of us. However, meteorologists (scientists who study the weather) want to know precisely how hot it is, how much it is raining, and from what direction the wind is blowing. Is it really freezing or is it just very cold? Meteorologists use many instruments to

Feeling a drop is enough to know that it is raining. But to find out *how much* rain there is, you will need to use weather instruments.

This meteorologist uses a weather instrument called an anemometer to measure the speed of the wind.

answer these questions. After learning about weather instruments, you can describe the weather just like a meteorologist!

COMPARE AND CONTRAST

Meteorology is the study of daily changes in weather in a particular place. Climatology is the study of the average weather conditions over long periods of time all over Earth. How are weather and climate similar? How are they different?

What Is the Temperature?

The thermometer is one of the oldest weather instruments still in use today. It measures temperature, or how hot or cold it is. The first thermometer was invented by an Italian scientist named Galileo in about 1592. Many different types of thermometers have been developed since then. The most basic type consists of a glass tube with liquid, called **mercury**, in it. Mercury expands when it heats up and shrinks when it cools down. These changes make the mercury level in the tube rise

Galileo did much more than invent the thermometer. He also used a telescope to make discoveries about space.

and fall. Markings on the outside of the tube show the degrees on a temperature scale.

There are several different scales that measure temperature. The two most common are Fahrenheit and Celsius. The Fahrenheit scale is used in the United States for everyday measurements. On this scale, the freezing point of water is 32 degrees and the boiling point is 212 degrees. The Celsius scale is used for scientific work and everyday weather measurements in much of the rest of the world. On this scale, the freezing point of water is 0 degrees and the boiling point is 100 degrees.

Cold? You can use a thermometer to tell when it is *literally* freezing.

Barometers

The atmosphere is the layer of gas that surrounds Earth. It is often called air. The weight of the air is called atmospheric, or barometric, pressure. Meteorologists use barometers to measure this pressure. The atmosphere is always moving and changing, and atmospheric pressure changes with it. These changes are associated with the weather.

Thunderstorms are caused by changes in atmospheric pressure, which is measured using a barometer.

FUN FACT

The barometer was invented in 1643 by Evangelista Torricelli, who worked with the Italian scientist Galileo shortly before Galileo died.

Following the changes in atmospheric pressure helps meteorologists predict changes in weather. If the pressure is falling, stormy weather is probably on the way. Rising pressure usually means the return of nice weather. When pressure remains steady, the weather will probably stay the same.

This barometer looks just like the one created by Evangelista Torricelli.

HYGROMETERS

Humidity is the amount of moisture in the air. It is the element of the atmosphere that changes most frequently. Meteorologists measure humidity with a device called a hygrometer. Simple hygrometers measure humidity by using a hair attached to a spring and dial. As the humidity increases, the hair gets shorter. This action pulls the spring and makes the dial hand move. When the humidity is lower, the hair is longer. This reaction loosens

Eighty percent humidity is pretty high. What kinds of places have high humidity?

Meteorologists report on many aspects of the weather, including humidity.

the tension on the spring and allows the dial hand to move in the other direction. Knowing the humidity helps meteorologists predict when it will rain or snow.

THINK ABOUT IT

Relative humidity is the amount of moisture in the air compared with the highest amount of moisture possible at the same temperature. A hot desert will have almost no relative humidity. However, a rain forest at the same temperature can have a very high relative humidity. What is the humidity like where you are today?

RAIN GAUGES

Meteorologists measure the amount of rain that falls with a rain gauge. Rain gauges are open-mouthed containers that catch rain as it falls. A typical rain gauge is made up of a measuring tube with a funnel on top. Meteorologists can tell how much it has rained by comparing the water level with the measurement marks on the container.

Another type of rain gauge is the tipping bucket rain gauge. This gauge automatically empties

You can use a rain gauge to tell if your garden is getting enough water.

It is important for farmers to have a precise understanding of rainfall patterns.

itself as the rain is measured. Knowing how much rain falls in an area helps farmers decide what crops to grow and when to plant and harvest them. Rain gauges also help scientists know when an area is getting too much or too little rain.

THINK ABOUT IT

Why is it important for scientists to know how much it rains in a particular area?

Wind Vanes

Studying wind is an important part of meteorology. The wind blowing around the world greatly affects climate and weather. Wind vanes (also known as weather vanes) tell us in which direction the wind is blowing. A simple wind vane is made of a piece of metal shaped like an arrow. The arrow turns until it faces the direction from which the wind is blowing. Winds are named for the direction from

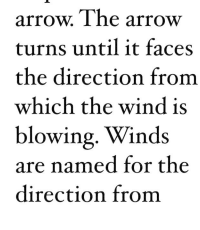

People put wind vanes on their houses to track the way the wind blows.

As it is often very windy at the beach, your hair can act as a kind of wind vane.

which they come. A wind that comes from the west is a west wind. Wind vanes help meteorologists track which way a storm is moving.

Think About It

Other than meteorologists, who else might want to know which way the winds are blowing?

ANEMOMETERS

Anemometers measure the speed of the wind. They look and work similar to wind vanes. In fact, many anemometers have wind vanes attached to them. An anemometer is made of three or four cups attached to the ends of arms. When the wind blows, it makes the anemometer spin. The faster the wind speed, the faster the anemometer turns. Meteorologists use anemometers to measure the strength of storms. Tropical storms have wind speeds of 39 miles (63 km) per hour or higher.

The cups on an anemometer catch the wind, which causes the arms to spin.

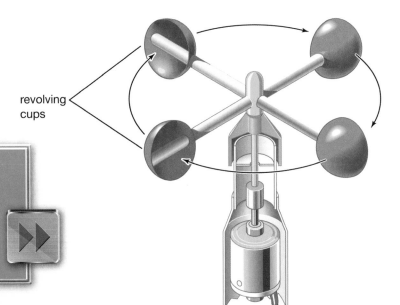

revolving cups

The violent winds of a tornado can flatten buildings and lift up heavy objects, such as cars, into the air.

A tropical storm becomes a hurricane when the wind speed goes over 74 miles (119 km) per hour. The wind speed of a tornado can reach as high as 300 miles (483 km) per hour.

THINK ABOUT IT

Why do you think that it's important for meteorologists to measure the power of storms using wind speed?

Weather Balloons and Radiosondes

Weather balloons were originally used to study wind patterns. A balloon was sent into the air and carried by wind currents. People on the ground used telescopes to study the speed and direction of the balloon at different **altitudes**. Meteorologists eventually wanted more

This weather balloon is being released from the end of an aircraft carrier to take atmospheric readings.

Here, a meteorologist is about to release a weather balloon with a radiosonde sensor into the air.

information on conditions higher up in the atmosphere. This desire led to the invention of the radiosonde in the late 1930s.

Radiosondes are collections of instruments that are attached to weather balloons. As the balloons rise, radiosondes record changes in air pressure, temperature, and humidity. This information is sent to the ground by radio. The balloons burst when they reach about 100,000 feet (30,000 meters) high. When that happens, the radiosonde is carried to the ground by parachute.

Altitude means height, particularly the height of something above sea level.

Ceilometers

A cloud is made up of millions of tiny water droplets or ice crystals floating together in the air. Meteorologists use ceilometers to measure the height of clouds. Ceilometers also measure the thickness of clouds. They shine a beam of light up at the clouds. The light is reflected from the clouds back to the ceilometer. Ceilometers use special telescopes to detect this reflection. Ceilometers can measure in

The three main types of clouds are cirrus (high and thin), cumulus (puffy), and stratus (layered). Can you guess which type of cloud is pictured here?

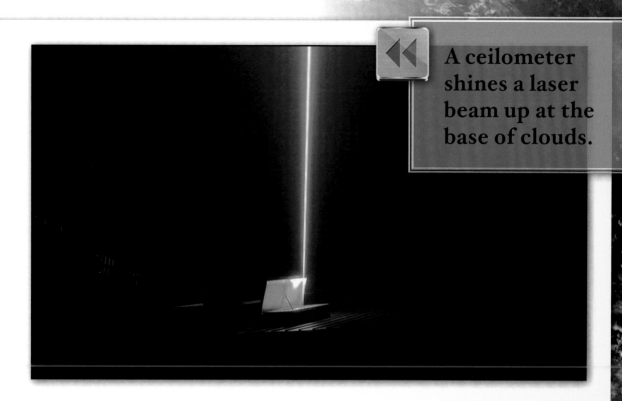

A ceilometer shines a laser beam up at the base of clouds.

the daytime or at night. Clouds often signal a weather change. Rising cloud levels mean the weather is clearing. Lower and thicker clouds mean it is going to rain.

THINK ABOUT IT

Ceilometers are used at airports to measure the base height of clouds. Why do you think it's important for an airport to know the height of clouds?

From the Telegraph to the Computer

The telegraph is a device for communicating. It uses electricity to send coded messages through wires. In the 1800s, the telegraph was the fastest way to communicate over long distances. It allowed scientists to collect and analyze data from many regions on Earth, including the oceans, deserts, and rain forests.

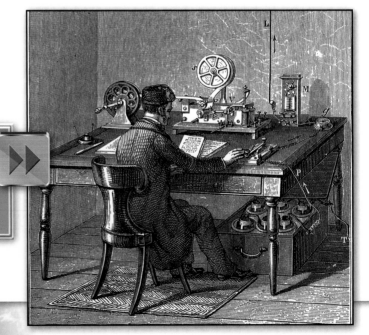

Operators used Morse code to send messages on electric telegraphs.

THINK ABOUT IT

The telegraph and computers made communicating about the weather much faster. Why do you think it's important to be able to communicate information about the weather quickly?

In the 1900s, computers became valuable tools in meteorology. They replaced the telegraph for communicating information about weather. Computer programs also use mathematics to create models of weather patterns. These models can reliably forecast the weather up to 30 days ahead of time.

Computers make communication about the weather much faster and more accurate than it was in the past.

WEATHER SATELLITES

The first weather **satellite** was launched into space in the 1960s. Weather satellites give meteorologists information about the atmosphere. Meteorologists use weather satellites to photograph weather systems, such as storms, around the world. This ability makes it possible for meteorologists to see changes in weather as soon as the changes happen.

Weather satellites provide photographs

Weather satellites orbit Earth in outer space.

This is a satellite image of a hurricane.

that make it possible to find and follow weather systems from the moment they form. Satellites also send lots of information on atmospheric conditions to scientists on the ground. Today, large storms are unlikely to strike without warning because weather satellites allow meteorologists to see them coming. Weather satellites make communicating about the weather faster than ever.

A **satellite** is a small object that revolves around a larger object in space. Satellites can be natural or made by humans.

Radar

Radar is a system that uses waves of energy to sense objects. Radar can find a faraway object and tell how fast it is moving. Radar units send radio waves, which are invisible streams of energy, into the air. When the waves hit an object, they bounce back to the radar unit. By measuring how long it takes the waves to return, the radar can tell how far away the object is. Radar can also tell

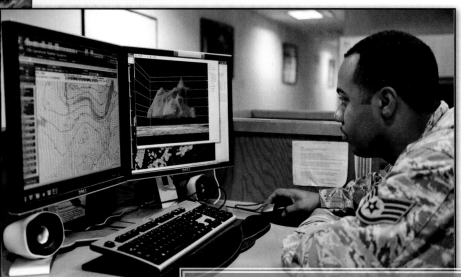

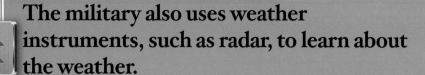
The military also uses weather instruments, such as radar, to learn about the weather.

Radar is used to track all kinds of weather, including lightning storms.

where a moving object is headed and at what speed. Sometimes it can tell how big objects are. Radar systems are one of the best ways to detect and track hurricanes, thunderstorms, tornadoes, and other powerful storms.

THINK ABOUT IT

Meteorologists use radar to track weather conditions. What other uses does radar have?

Do It Yourself!

Meteorologists use many instruments to measure, predict, and talk about the weather. But they are not the only people who use weather instruments. You can use an outdoor thermometer and barometer to keep track of the temperature and atmospheric pressure in your neighborhood. Home-improvement stores sell inexpensive hygrometers that you can use to measure the humidity in your garden or right outside your window. And you can easily make a rain gauge, a wind vane, and an anemometer

You can use weather instruments to do science experiments in school.

THINK ABOUT IT

Weather stations are places built for taking, recording, and reporting information about weather. Why is it important to do all of these things in one place?

yourself! You may have some trouble getting your hands on a radiosonde or a ceilometer, but you can definitely attach a helium balloon to a long string and use it as a miniature weather balloon. You can even use the Internet to see satellite images from space and track weather patterns on radar! But be careful. Weather conditions can be dangerous, especially if there is lightning around.

These students use a rain gauge to see how much water their plants are getting.

GLOSSARY

altitude The height of something above the level of the sea.

atmosphere The layer of gas that surrounds Earth.

atmospheric pressure The weight of the air.

climate The long-term weather conditions of any place.

climatology The study of the average weather conditions over long periods of time all over Earth.

degree A unit for measuring temperature.

humidity The amount of moisture in the air.

hurricane An extremely large, powerful, and destructive storm with very strong winds.

instrument A device that measures something (such as temperature or distance).

meteorologists People who study and predict weather.

meteorology The study of daily changes in weather in a particular place.

Morse code A system of electronic communication that uses dots, dashes, and spaces to represent letters, punctuation, and numbers. The symbols are arranged to spell out a message.

predict To make a guess about something that might happen.

tornado A storm in which powerful rotating winds form a column, which reaches from a cloud down toward the ground.

tropical storm A powerful storm that begins over warm tropical oceans and that has winds that are not as strong as those of a hurricane.

weather stations Places built for taking, recording, and reporting information about weather.

For More Information

Books

Arlon, Penelope. *Weather* (Discover More). New York, NY: Scholastic, 2013.

Bredeson, Carmen. *Weird but True Weather.* Berkeley Heights, NJ: Enslow Elementary, 2011.

Mogil, H. Michael, and Barbara G. Levine. *Extreme Weather.* New York, NY: Simon and Schuster, 2011.

Rattini, Kristin Baird. *Weather*. Washington, DC: National Geographic Society, 2013.

Snedeker, Joe. *The Everything Kids' Weather Book*. Avon, MA: Adams Media, 2012.

Websites

Because of the changing nature of Internet links, Rosen Publishing has developed an online list of websites related to the subject of this book. This site is updated regularly. Please use this link to access the list:

http://www.rosenlinks.com/LFO/Instr

INDEX

CANCELLED